SCOOTERS

WHEELS IN MOTION

Morgan Hughes

Rourke

Publishing LLC

Vero Beach, Florida 32964

www.rourkepublishing.com

PHOTO CREDITS: Cover, p 10, 12, 13, 17, 18 courtesy of RazorUSA; title page Scott Peterson/Getty Images; p 4 Chris Hondros/Getty Images; p 7, 8, 21 Pat McBeth

Title page: *You're never too young to start enjoying the fun of scootering.*

Editor: Frank Sloan

Cover design by Nicola Stratford

Library of Congress Cataloging-in-Publication Data

Hughes, Morgan, 1957-
 Scooters / Morgan Hughes.
     v. cm. — (Wheels in motion)
Includes bibliographical references and index.
Contents: Scooters in the beginning — Getting started — Get to know your scooter — Tricks — Motors vs. self-propelled — Streets and parks — Team razor — Equipment and repairs — Safety tips.
  ISBN 1-58952-667-8 (hardcover)
 1. Scootering—Juvenile literature. 2. Scooters—Juvenile literature. [1. Scooters.] I. Title. II. Series: Hughes, Morgan, 1957-   Wheels in motion.

 GV859.77.H84 2003
 796.6—dc21

                                                    2003004041

Printed in the USA

CG/CG

Table of Contents

Scooters in the Beginning

Scooters made of wood have been around for many years. But the modern **aluminum** version was actually devised by the head of a bicycle manufacturing company. He wanted an easier way to get around exhibits when he was attending sporting goods shows!

When the reindeer are away, Santa turns to alternate transportation.

Getting Started

Like any wheeled sport, scootering takes some getting used to. Balance is the key. The horizontal handlebars offer a good visual measure for how upright you are. Plant one foot squarely in the middle of the riding deck. Next, **propel** yourself by pushing forward with the other foot and then gliding.

Just starting out? Make sure to go slowly and wear protective pads.

Get to Know Your Scooter

A successful scooterer will learn about the machine and its parts. The **frame** includes the handlebars and T-tube, then the tube clamp and the steerer tube. Near the bottom are the joint lever and front fork. Along the deck are the rear break wheel guard and wheel bracket.

Most scooters have a quick-release clamp so you can adjust handlebar height.

9

Tricks

Bicycling, in-line skating, and skateboarding have special tricks. So does the scooter crowd. Among the most popular: the Nosewheelie, the Slanted Grind, and the Ollie Manual. Before long, you too can be jumping, spinning, twisting, and hopping your scooter all over the neighborhood.

Scooters have joined the parade of "rad" sports with extreme stunts.

Look ma...no feet!

The sheer delight of getting airborne comes after you master the basics.

Motors vs. Self-propelled

In addition to the aluminum scooter, the self-propelled scooter has been joined by a host of others. Some even have small engines attached, making them into "stand-up motorcycles." The **motorized** machines aren't meant to go very fast, but they are a fun way to scoot around the neighborhood.

You can get around town with a motorized scooter and never break a sweat.

Streets and Parks

There is no holding back the scooter **enthusiast** when it comes to showing off and copying the tricks of skateboarders and in-line skaters. They use ramps and **half-pipes** and bowls. Scooterers are quickly becoming the next thing in **extreme** wheeled sports, both in specially designed parks and in the streets.

Skate parks draw scooterers who want to join in the tricks and stunts.

Team Razor

Team Razor is a group of skilled **professional** riders. They have taken all the tricks they learned on skateboards, BMX bikes, and in-line skates and applied them to scooters with a style all their own. They practice and perform all over the country at skate parks, in neighborhoods, and at various events.

Team Razor travels the country, showing off and sharing the fun.

Equipment and Repairs

Like any machine, your scooter will work better and last longer if you take good care of it. One way is to keep dirt out of the wheels and make sure the rear wheel brake hood is not clogged with mud, grass, or other things. You can use many of the same products designed for bike maintenance on your scooter.

Fly higher and farther with clean, well-maintained gear.

Safety Tips

Even though you're not attached to your scooter as you are to, say, in-line skates, you can still fall off. It is best always to wear a helmet, particularly when you're mastering basic skills. Elbow and knee protection, too, is a good idea and will keep you from getting discouraged—or worse—in the early stages.

Glossary

aluminum (ah LOOM uh num) — a strong, lightweight metal used in bike and scooter frames

enthusiast (en THOOZ ee ast) — someone who is very involved with a particular subject or activity

extreme (ECKS TREEM) — beyond the normal, expected level; very intense

frame (FRAYM) — the system of tubing that acts as a bike's or scooter's skeleton

half-pipes (HAFF PYPZ) — cross-sections of a tube used for gaining speed and taking air

motorized (MOH tur IYZD) — powered by an engine

professional (pro FESH uh nul) — a person who performs a job or a skill for pay

propel (PRO PELL) — to cause to move or maintain motion

Index

Further Reading

Bibbins, Neil. *Bikes, Scooters, Skates, and Boards*. Storey Books
     Publishing, 2002
Case, Jeremy and Zac Sandler. *Scooters: The Ultimate Guide*. Aladdin
     Library, 2001
Rosenberg, Aaron. *Razor Scooter: Rad Sports*. Rosen Publishing Group, 2003
Schlesinger, W., et al. *Scooter Mania*. St. Martin's Press, 2000

Websites To Visit

www.razorusa.com/
www.scooter-info.com/
www.razor-scooter.com/

About The Author

Morgan Hughes is the author of more than 50 books on hockey, track and
field, bicycling, and many other subjects. He is also an avid cyclist and professional
musician currently living with his family in Connecticut.